T0158786

**Also by Kirk DeMatas**

*Wordspeak* (2008)

# Conversations with Skeletons

## Kirk DeMatas

iUniverse, Inc.
Bloomington

# Conversations with Skeletons

*iUniverse books may be ordered through booksellers or by contacting:*

*iUniverse*
*1663 Liberty Drive*
*Bloomington, IN 47403*
*www.iuniverse.com*
*1-800-Authors (1-800-288-4677)*

*Because of the dynamic nature of the Internet, any web addresses or links contained in this book may have changed since publication and may no longer be valid. The views expressed in this work are solely those of the author and do not necessarily reflect the views of the publisher, and the publisher hereby disclaims any responsibility for them.*

*Any people depicted in stock imagery provided by Thinkstock are models, and such images are being used for illustrative purposes only.*

*Certain stock imagery © Thinkstock.*

*ISBN: 978-1-4759-3424-3 (sc)*
*ISBN: 978-1-4759-3423-6 (e)*

*Library of Congress Control Number: 2012911173*

*Printed in the United States of America*

*iUniverse rev. date: 7/5/2012*

**For**

**Myriam, Arthur, Samuel, and Joseph**

# Contents

# Introduction

*There is something about a closet that
makes a skeleton terribly restless.*

—Wilson Mizner, Playwright.

In the autumn of 2008, a dear friend of mine told me that her marriage was coming to an end. She was heartbroken. She had poured so much of her love and herself into this relationship, and now she, wearing her love for this man as a badge of honour, was thrust into a world of mourning. It hurt to see her suffer, and so we began to spend more time together. She became my sister, her children became my nephews, and I became their guard dog. I watched as she grieved for the loss of her relationship. I watched as she searched within for the strength to move forward in her life. I watched as she travelled back into her past to confront her demons. I watched her walk in confidence on a path toward a future full of light.

One night, while spending time with my friend and her children, I came to the realization that my own closet had become cluttered with painful memories. I had to accept that in order for me to become a strong and positive influence for my friend, her children, and anyone else in my life, I too would have to travel back into my past to confront my demons.

I started writing poems for this book in December 2008, and at the time, I told another dear friend that I could complete this project in two weeks. I did not realize then that this project would demand that I unearth my soul in order to reveal the skeletons buried within. Each poem in this collection is a recollection and reenactment of an experience, and so each poem is presented in chronological order. For the past three and a half years, I regularly positioned myself in a figurative place of darkness in order to converse with each memory. I communicated with my former selves as if they were individuals. I tried to understand their pain. I cannot even describe the intensity of the emotions that met me in those private moments. I often felt as if I were losing my mind to the hungry wilderness of the past. I came close to abandoning this project so many times; however, upon the completion of each poem, I was rewarded with a sense of relief, swiftly followed by an exquisite feeling of accomplishment for casting out another demon.

The majority of the poetry in this collection was written in free verse; however, I did experiment with different types of poetry, such as the Ronsard ode ("Ode to My Present"), the terza rima ("Into the Arms of Fate"), and the traditional Welsh triban ("Adam and Angie"). I flirted with different rhyme schemes, such as the Venus and Adonis ("As the Godfather Rises and Sets") and the ballad ("My Eyes Would Rather Scrape the Floor"). I also decided to bastardize certain types of metre, such as the Alexandrine ("Confronting the Grief of Years").

To further enhance the experience of this book for myself and for you, the reader, I asked my good friend Tosin, president of TIA International Photography, to be the chief photographer for this project. The poetry in this collection erupted from an intimate and often emotionally chaotic place, so it was important to me that I work with a skillful photographer I could trust. My defences were lowered for four days as Tosin captured over four thousand photos from seven photo shoots. It was definitely a challenge to choose only eighteen photos for this book.

It is my belief that exposing demons to the light diminishes their power. Freedom reigns in the distance, but it all begins with a few conversations with skeletons.

Kirk DeMatas
Toronto, June 12, 2012

# I. A Boy's Miseducation

# Confronting the Grief of Years

On my thirtieth birthday, I woke to the sound
of bones rattling inside my closet.
The vibrations rapped against my naked eardrums
and lured me into the realm of the blues.
My consciousness rode the sound waves like a sea bird
scanning an abyss for some nourishment.
Beguiled by this rhythm, I understood the trap,
just as Josef K. does in *The Trial*.[1]
I could hear the scratching against the heavy door,
and after what felt like one year, I stood.
My hand became a benevolent dictator,
ushering the darkness into the light.
The air was soaked in the miasma of secrets
exhaled by the shadows in my closet.
Frozen in the eye of a tornado, I watched
as secret histories swirled about me.
I recognized my various incarnations
caught in their repetitious narrations.
My former selves remained the monarchs in their worlds;
as I witnessed this, I became anguished.
To save my former selves, I had to dry my tears;
I confronted the grief of many years.
The light of peace filled the room and I became free.

---

1 Franz Kafka published a novel titled *The Trial* in 1925. The story focused on
Josef K., a chief financial officer of a bank. The morning of his thirtieth birthday,
Josef awakes to authorities placing him under arrest for an unspecified crime.

# As the Godfather Rises and Sets

Your eyes shine as bright as two sunrises
in the old photo housed in its frame,
a picture of love from another time,
when innocence was not met with shame.
My mind travels into this charming scene
to embrace my cherished memories.

Your eyes shine as bright as two sunrises
as you fetch me from a night of dreams.
My young tongue trips over words as I cry
over night visions of beasts and fiends.
Wrapped up in your arms, I sleep as in bed;
creatures dare not creep into my head.

Your eyes shine as bright as two sunrises
in my mind as I try to hold on.
The image of you slips into the sky,
and time seems to roll back to the dawn.
The night returns, and I fall back asleep;
the beasts return to me—in my dreams.

Your eyes whisper farewell as two sunsets
ride into the opened arms of night.
My tongue trips over my words as I fret
over the loss of my own white knight.
Wrapped up in the distractions of strange men,
I wish I could see your face again.

# Sophismata

The innocents lay in the arms of darkness;
resting comfortably in the silence,
the two fall into a deep slumber.

In dreams, the young silhouettes enjoy
the pleasantries of the fantastical.
The sun runs along their skin
as laughter rides upon the wind;
they are free from the seduction
of ripened fears.

But even in this dreamland, the sun
must fall, and as the night draws near,
the innocents are steered back to reality.

Quiet in the room, the silence is startled
by her harsh voice. Staring and not seeing,
her vision is twisted by a suspicious imagination.

Accusations simmer behind her hot eyes.
She burns my innocence away, and I rot,
the memory of me swiftly banished
into the shadows of her mind.

---

2 *Sophismata* is a Latin term that refers to ambiguity, as well as what is determined to be true or false about this ambiguity based upon the interpretation that is placed upon it.

# SHADOW GAMES

My schoolboy self hangs
his head in shame.
He stares at his feet, now engaged
in an adult game,
one he does not understand
but feels compelled to play.
A muffled voice whispers
into my right ear,
just as an unknown shadow
comes into the light —
a head juts out, and I respond
in spite of my fear.
Delighted by the company
and curious about the presence of he,
whose face remains hidden from me,
I enter willingly, as he unknowingly
breaks the rules to play with me.
Staring at his feet, my eyes sail upward
and I see what would later attract me.
The stranger ends this round of the game,
but not before sparking my curiousity.
My schoolboy self hangs
his head in shame.

# Halder Crescent Crush

I see the feet scrambling past the basement window.
Immediately and discreetly,
my fresh fascination with blasphemy awakes
and tugs at me.
Silence floods the concrete-walled space
and plugs my ears.
All I hear is the sound of my heart beating,
rapidly speeding to accommodate the thoughts
racing in my mind.
This blazing and sudden heat incites me
to cool myself with a honey-sweet treat.

I run up the stairs and open the door;
there before me stands the neighbourly governor—
the one of my adolescent fantasies.
I look at you—you are unassuming.
You are unaware of the magnificence of you
leaping right into me.
My heart races to match the rush
of the bloody stampede.
My head is open to countless pictures of you.
The sorcery of lust binds me.
I serve blindly, even as fear invades,
even as I wish I could succumb to cowardice;
I am led by the need for a kiss.

Impetuous youth—I am choosing
not to associate consequences with my actions.
I soften my resolve and my defence strategy
to be one with my curiosity.
I choose to embrace my burgeoning lasciviousness.
The knock on the door quickly becomes a rumble.
Thunder grumbles within me; hunger wraps
itself around my sensibility.
The helpless one is squeezed into complacency.
I open the door.

We quietly sneak into a cemented room nearby.
The faint scent of gasoline lends
a dirty flavour to the seduction scene.
Locked in the darkness,
with nervousness in abundance,
we begin to caress each other.
I think to myself that my parents hoped
I would turn out better than this.
Shaken suddenly by a kiss,
we are both paralyzed.
A witness was born in the eyes
of my sister.

# Scraps in Your Eyes

I feel your menacing eyes pierce
through my fragile exterior.
Behind my meagre defences,
you now see that the core of me
harbours a so-called deformity.
You are disgusted that I would permit
a freak to seek tenancy within me.
You demand an explanation.
You suspect premeditation.
You suspect that I pursued this liaison.
Your assumptions lead to your revulsion.
I feel you shun your firstborn son,
even as I deny ownership of this aberration.
I am cast out of your sight.
I am left disarmed and vulnerable to harm.
I am set as a feast to be devoured
by the most wicked beast.
I am scraps thrown to my new kin.

# Warfare

Bedtime shadows whisper into my ears;
words sound like wicked weapons.

Shrapnel explodes violently inside;
wounds open their gaping mouths.

I lie awake, a bloodstained battlefield;
warriors do not stand by.

I stare up at the naked sky of night;
lone soldier will fight again.

# I Paint Bruises

The day holds its breath as I breeze
into my parents' room.
I am sullen;
I am a slave to the blackness
colouring me inside.
A schism brought my internal counsel
to its knees, stripping me of the confidence
needed to clip the wings of a rising tide.
No confidants left;
they were victims of theft.

So I invade this space,
aware of what awaits—a case laced
with rainbow bait for the face.
The colours, in all their glimmering glory,
dance in my eyes.
I am left temporarily mystified,
but I quickly disarm my innocent fascination
and submit to my inauspicious inclination.

The day holds its breath, watching
as I formulate my resolution.
I seek an exposition.
I am tired of my anonymity.
My eyes stare intensely
at the peculiar case;
the colours mean nothing to me;
I want the absence of this.
I dip my fingers into the blackness,
swirling throughout the darkness
of this compact sea.
I paint the bruises around my eyes,
drowning them in lies,
to reveal the anger inside.
I stand before the mirror—hypnotized.
I am now ready for the inquisition.

# II. A Youth's Discovery

# When Lambs Feast on Forbidden Fruit

The light from the moon pools
on the cold mansard roof
before raining down upon us—
three Christian lambs.
We wear the moonlight briefly
before it melts off
into the night,
then coolly walk
into the light
of the faux Art Deco lobby.
This hotel,
in all its majesty,
with its coat of arms,
impresses the elite,
but not us—
the youths wrapped in jeans.

The hotel porter shepherds us
through the eerie hallway.
The yellow paint languishes
on the walls;
our feet grind hard
into the soft green floors,
and the air vents call out to us
with one collective hiss,
that bliss will come
once we enter the pit.
All of this mingles
in my mind,
conjuring up a terrifying image
of us sliding down the throat
of a snake—
we reach the pit.

As we enter our room,
the butterflies in my stomach
grow dragon-sized wings.
I stand still, almost paralyzed

as I stare at the bed built for kings.
Anxious to drown my nervousness,
anxious to begin our celebration,
liquor of various colours pours
out of our bags
and into us.
We soak up the spirits,
pushing our limits,
becoming senseless,
as we fill the room
with youthful nonsense.
The playground becomes us.

Lost in the bliss of drunkenness,
we dare the universe to master us,
and with just one kiss,
temptation devours our piousness.
We bathe in the sweetness
of forbidden fruit,
relishing the moment
before its juices wash away.
The sun charges into our room unexpectedly
to light our embarrassed faces.
We cover ourselves;
we hide ourselves;
we shield our semi-nude bodies,
hoping to bury in sheets
the joy of rolling in the sweat
of each other.

# İ, Asmodaeus

This mirror frames my changing universe.
My effigy stares blankly before shattering
into pieces. My remains dissolve
into ripples within the sea of glass.
Staring into this silent chaos, I
see somebody rise from the ground of me.

A suit of shadows clings tightly to his body;
his face resembles my own, but his eyes
carry a darkness that I do not own.
I want to shield my soul from his vision
but the mystery that creeps behind his eyes
intrigues me, and leads me down to his lips.

His dusk-kissed mouth opens like a nimbus cloud
and his long red tongue falls down to his waist.
His words rain down and swiftly pierce my soul;
I taste his persuasion all over me.
I watch him happily crawl in the filth
of his manifested imagination.

The spirit of lust drips from his willing lips
as a starless night hollows out his eyes.
He incites me to rest beneath his sky
so that I can freely fantasize.
I taste his passion as I lick my lips.
I surrender to my new compulsion.

The elixir I seek springs forth from many,
and I watch as shadows roll over me.
There is no stranger standing in place.
In the mirror, I only see my face.
The spirit of lust drips from my lips
as a joyless night hollows out my eyes.

---

3 Asmodaeus is a king of demons featured in the deuterocanonical Book of
Tobit. He is also known as the demon of lust responsible for twisting people's
sexual desires.

# The Jaws of Temptation

Temptation's handmaiden lays a veil over my mind;
I am covered by a universe free from the gravity
of a prudish mankind.

Curiosity blasts me into this space but not before
social decency can tether itself to my body;
I fly as if in a dream but remain awake.

My heart thumps wildly in my throat and beats
itself against the cage; I swallow the beat
as it rages to the tune of my conscience.

The beat falls to its knees within me and kneels
in the pit of my stomach; I feel my anxious heart
rock like a nervous ship on an angry sea.

Amorous eyes melt and drip like candles and bind
to me like wax to a wrist; I choose to be helpless,
and I choose to be devoured.

Temptation opens its jaws and swallows my spirit;
I sink into this moment of carnal truth and kneel
in its pit. I rock myself in the stomach of lust.

# Chimera

Like a diamond in God's eye,
the moon shines; its light covers
the sleeping Earth.

The moon watches from afar,
as we drift freely
through the sea of night.

Our souls shine like newborn stars,
unaccustomed to the dark,
unaccustomed to our light.

Tonight, she speaks softly,
though her words are far too heavy
to be carried away by the night air.

She falls like a divine being,
sinking from the heavens
into my earthly soul.

She, loving me like a soul mate,
charges forward like a saint,
to save me from my dark fate.

She carries her truth like a candle;
the sparks throw light into my shadows,
revealing an antiquated field of battle.

My sanity loses its footing,
plunging me into the ghastly mouth
of the chimera.

Swallowed by this fantasy,
my humanity watches as two armies vie
for spiritual supremacy.

The soul in me steadies the battle land
to carry the force of The Lion:
he who walks with a mane of lambs.

The soul in me dusts the land like a mantle,
seducing the greedy eyes of the wolf:
he who skulks with a cloak of jackals.

I watch helplessly as my light flickers,
bending and twisting to the will
of the ones lost in their bitter war.

I blow out the flame and watch
as her truth dissipates,
waiting for the night to consume me.

# My Eyes Would Rather Scrape the Floor

I stand before you, hopelessly humbled
by the foul stench of my shame.
You sit before me, clearly crumbling
under the weight of your disgrace.

The room is saturated with silence
as we mourn the passing of love.
We bow our heads; we seek forgiveness;
we abhor what we have become.

My eyes lift and fall deep into your gaze;
I find myself locked in a trance.
I am lifted from Earth into your space
to witness our doomed romance.

The universe hastily stirs the stars
into wicked constellations.
Feuding lovers, now feuding beasts at war,
charge toward their own destruction.

The constellation of Cancer, I am
the crab tearing into your hide.
The constellation of Aries, you ram
into the shell where my soul hides.

We madly endeavour to win this fight;
we lose, which ignites the last spark,
and we explode into fiery light,
before melting into the dark.

Our universe now mangled by war,
broken stars are all that remain.
I lower my head; my eyes scrape the floor;
I cannot bear to see this pain.

# Fistful of Memories

Staring into my open hands,
I see that my palms
like the Hakra riverbed
are stained with your tears—
my former Ghaggar River.[4]

I remember ...

You used to rush over me with love;
your Hakka tongue caressed
every word that slipped
into me.

The new millennium gave birth
to my love revolution, and so
I wrapped myself around you.
Like a planet spinning around
the axis of you,
I allowed both the light and the dark
to consume me.

You led me into manhood.
You led me into sex.
You led me into love,
and we devoured each other
to create our paradise.
We did a disservice to ourselves
to serve an ideal.
We ignored the tremors rumbling
beneath the surface;
and as the foundation ruptured,
a gaping hole licked its lips
before sucking us in.

---

4  The Ghaggar-Hakra River is an intermittent river in India and Pakistan that
only flows during the monsoon season.

There we were,
trapped in the belly of madness,
yielding to savagery,
biting into each other with words;
this verbal slaughter exhausted us
and left us lost in the hotness
of irrational fury.
We watched our love slowly mutate
into hate.

These memories no longer occupy
my mind's watchful eye.
My interest in this evaporates
like mist.
My ten fingers curl and lock;
my two fists, hard as rocks,
cannot be penetrated.
We are no more.

# Into the Arms of Fate

*For Phil*

The city sidewalk soaks up the night rain
as the people push each other aside;
they seem accustomed to their busy pace.

They cannot imagine his gutter life.
He crawled into a vagrant for shelter
after misfortune had swallowed his pride.

Stationed eagerly upon the church stairs;
his outstretched arm opens a starving hand.
The busy people have no coins to share.

Their gentle smiles occasionally land
like droplets of sunlight upon his face;
warmth temporarily covers this man.

Rising to his feet, he submits to faith
and walks into the opened arms of fate.

# I Watch, and Deep Down, I Repent

Holy water sweats from my temples;
it retreats from a tainted house.
The chalice in my heart is barren;
its womb was emptied of all guilt.
Gutted to serve a foreign agent,
an emissary of torment,
a bite from an invisible beast
initiates the invasion.
I hear the new chapel bells ringing;
the chalice is full of jewels.
I am numb, a slave to the venom,
and I am now its instrument.
A demon set loose upon my words;
I watch, and deep down, I repent.
It runs with the speed of a cheetah;
I watch, and deep down, I repent.
It stalks prey like a cunning jaguar;
I watch, and deep down, I repent.
It spits its darkness into your light;
I watch, and deep down, I repent.
My friend, a witness to my plight,
sits in silence.

# Adam and Angie

The disappearance of my love
stirs the stink of anguish
into my heart.

Rapt by the sorrow spiraling
down to the depths, I plunge deep
into the mess within myself.

Drowning in the shadows cast
by my absent love, I thirst
for the warmth of solace.

With perfectly timed swiftness,
two misfit spirits named Adam and Angie
call me to the surface.

Adam, skittish and delirious,
promises me deliverance,
if I choose to taste his bliss.

Angie, light and full of delight,
assures me that I can be free,
if I leap into her white sea.

In my weakness, I accept their kindness;
I allow them to caress and
comfort my wounded heart.

I lose control in this moment,
soon becoming infected
with their delicious art.

Visions bleed before my eyes and
explode like stars in the sky,
before melting into my mind.

I feel the universe flying inside;
the memories of my absent love
quickly fade and die.

The next morning, a new pain reigns.
My body sweats; my heart frets,
and I grieve again.

# When a Virgin Spring Falls

You are like a virgin spring
falling into a new world.

Glowing with such purity,
you attract fake gallantry.

You choose to dilute yourself
with the mire around you.

I watch as your shine grows dull;
I watch as you become me.

# III. A Man's Awakening

# BLOOD

I step away from the scene of us engaged
in a thundering vocal exchange.
I seek cover from the fall of acidic rain
before guilt washes over me again.
I slip into the basement, immersing myself
in silence. I am unable to squelch the echo
of past emotional violence. I am helpless,
stricken by sudden paralysis; memories beat
inside my heart like drums. History cries
in the wilderness, desperately searching
for a release from this emptiness.
My blood rushes.

I contemplate returning to the scene to voice
my apologies, but I am frozen in place.
I am unable to erase the bitter taste dripping
from my tongue; my pride keeps me stubborn.
My kin rolls above me like dark clouds before a storm;
hanging over me, he feels heavy. I listen
as his tongue treads softly. I watch
as his eyes rage uncontrollably.
His fingers grow into sharp blades and glide
across the icy surface of his skin.
I shout out for my kin.
His blood rushes.

Screams rush over us like stormy waves, crashing
and pouring gallons of panic into us.
We quiver like shallow glass jars, on the verge
of shattering into pieces on the floor.
I hold her as if she were my child. I listen
as she wraps her prayers in tears. I watch
as her tears defy gravity and climb to heaven.
Light breaks through the clouds and streams
into each of us. Remnants of darkness evaporate
and disappear, and it seems like all is clear.
We are told to hold this story near.
Our blood rushes.

# GRAVE RAPTURE

We slip into robes made of shadows
and roll like mist into the night.
We willfully masquerade as anti-heroes
to release our obscene fantasies.
Our disturbed moralities take control
and drop us into a consecrated bed.
We claw into each other like animals;
like brutes of nature, we pierce deep
into our fading humanities.
One last kiss frees life from our lips,
and we watch as our spirits orgasm
amongst the dead.

# Falsus Amor

The foundation we built has dissolved
into sand; I stand alone with only grains
of us strewn across my opened hand.

My eyes appraise these morsels of love,
then follow closely as they are lifted
above, by the whims of eager winds.

A voice rides on the back of a breeze;
it calls my eyes out to sea; serendipity
it seems, stands tall and waits for me.

Heartache blinds me so I cannot see that he
who stands on the water is not a saviour
for me; a swamp sucks at his feet.

This lover draws me easily into his waters;
I fail to see that I have forsaken myself
to drown beneath his feet.

---

5 *Falsus* is Latin for mistaken (or by extension: fake or untrue). *Amor* is Latin
for love.

# SHOWER

The colour of you rains blue nails
over my wooden and naked body.
Memories drop into me, hammering
every moment deep into me, forcing
me to scream out in anguish.
You continue to wash over me,
tempting me to rub you into me.
I clutch myself tightly to keep you
close, but I feel you quickly slip
between my fingers. I watch you bleed
and land at my feet. I look down and wish
you could crawl into me one last time.

# Eyes Devour Me

Your eyes crawl over me
like vermin over a lifeless body.
Your eyes scavenge for the last
grains of me. You are autocratic;
crawling over me and settling in
as if my body was a colony.
Your eyes are hungry; they devour me
as if driven mad by blinding gluttony.
They feed off my body to suffocate
your insecurities. A demonized shape
is all that remains and it is covered
entirely by you.

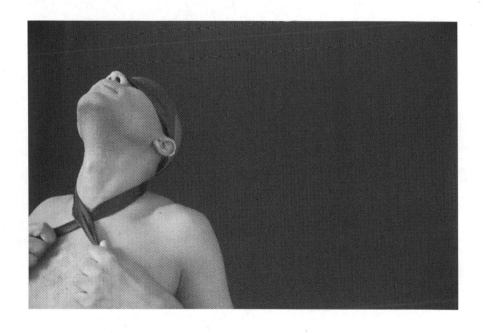

# Siren

Your lonely body sings beautifully
and like a siren, you soon seduce me.

Your voice dances above the hungry waves;
I steer myself toward the sound I crave.

Your notes spill into my soul with such ease,
I do not see the danger seizing me.

I begin to drown in the sound of you.
No one can save me from my chosen doom.

# Virtual Love

*For Nick M.*

Millions of bits of microchips congregate
within a man-made electronic space;
Communicating with sparks like new lovers,
they create a virtual universe.

Possibility melts into an ocean;
the curious swim with outstretched fingers.
Travelling into the realm of what can be,
eyes feed on luscious opportunities.

I join the masses for this bountiful feast;
surfing through galaxies until I reach
the undiscovered space wrapped all around you;
I swiftly dock myself next to your feet.

We walk in unison and watch as Change rolls
multiple worlds up into its cloaked fists.
The crushed planets bleed into one another
as we quickly walk away from this sight.

Our shared audacity blinds us easily
to the same change planning to conquer us.
We break the natural laws to write our love
into the gravity within our space.

We push ourselves deep into this chosen core
and sacrifice all logic and reason.
We construct a shared destiny as our home
and live as if this life is eternal.

In our private bliss, we both fail to notice
the door to our house open like a wound;
It broadcasts a hesitant invitation
to the unsatisfied beast that is Change.

Sinking into the room like a deep shadow
diligently stalking a lit candle,
Change pursues the light upon our bright faces.
We are not impermeable planets.

Change drinks of our spirits; our life force soon dries.
We drift apart and fade into the dark.
Gravity retires, sending memories
into the arms of antiquated stars.

# Grave Dance

I stand on the subway platform
beset by my demon shadows.
The fierce crowd scratches at my flesh.
Startled, I run right to the edge.
I peer into the iron trench
as memories howl for the end.
My eyes run along the slick tracks
like hungry rats searching for scraps.
The dark tunnel swallows my eyes
and briefly silences my mind.
In this crypt, peace flows into me
like wine, so intoxicating.
Suddenly, headlights flood my eyes
and I am thrown back into time.

My hands grip the ends of the sink
as I stare at the harmful drink.
The fear of my supposed fate
leads me to swallow my escape.
The poisoned cocktail burns my throat,
but fails to fulfill my dark hope.

A flash of light paints a new scene:
I lie awake, roused from my sleep.
My eyes are bloodshot and bleary,
my body robbed by lethargy.
A microscope cannot see me;
the pills swim inside lazily.

A flash lights up another place:
The Prince Edward bridge calls my name.
I walk, as if trapped in a trance,
asking for one last morbid dance.
My body prepares to release,
but a kind stranger intervenes.

These memories take leave from me;
I return to the present gladly.
Darkness melts away from my sight.
I no longer see the headlights.
I stand on the subway platform
escorted by just one shadow.

# Truth as a Main Course

My need to please exposes an old wound:
Unattended since youth, it now consumes,
strangling my words into submission. I
taste bitterness as I spit pleasantries.
Angelic One, you know me and see me.
Recognizing my false agreements, you
dare me to see the truth, to heal myself.

# Root

My fingers mature into claws, hooking
themselves into the ground and digging
into its back, like lover's flesh.

I tunnel down, travelling deep into the core
until I reach the truth. Buried within me,
a single root thrives, with my history

swirling in its rings, like blood in veins,
running cyclically until the truth boils
and the root bursts to the surface.

# GROWTH

You drift into me like the breath of the sea,
purifying the scant land of me.
You plant the seed for a new tree
and it grows relentlessly.
It brings me up with a source of strength,
growing until I finally wake,
growing until I reach the floating lake.
The lightest parts of me, learn*ed* and imbued
with memory, fly away and upward
like leaves, gliding through the air.
I rejoice in the gift of transformation.

# Ode to My Present

My present breaks free from the hollow past
    like a monarch from its cocoon.
The wings of possibility so vast
    rise above the world like the moon,
        lighting the night that once took flight inside
        my tender spirit. I decide

to savour the sweet nectar of instants.
    Life is milkweed before my eyes
awaiting assured consumption by chance;
    my evolution surprises:
        I define a refined state of being;
        I become all that is freeing.

# Acknowledgments

My most sincere gratitude and appreciation goes to my angels: Myriam Glémot, Arthur Diesen, Samuel Diesen, and Joseph Diesen. Thank you for inspiring me to write this book.

Thanks to my parents and my aunt Janet for the support and unconditional love.

My eternal gratitude goes out to my dear friend and big brother Tosin I. Arasi (TIA International Photography) for agreeing to be the chief photographer for this project. Thank you for accompanying me on this journey and for bringing Alphie with us.

Extra special thanks to my friends: Alain Brazeau, Cathryn Naiker, Byron Pappas, Sara Carvalho, and Simone Maurice. Thank you for giving so freely and for venturing so completely into this project. Special thanks to Cathryn for the beautiful make-up; Al for becoming my male model; and Greg for suggesting the Davisville bridge and the sunglasses.

Thanks to iUniverse for giving me another chance to explore my imagination. Special thanks to Krista Hill, Ben Hudson, Jamie Mitchell, Olive S. and Allison Howell.

Extra special thanks to Byron Pappas and Gregory Jones for reviewing my manuscript. Thanks for your honesty.

Thanks to Anthony and Creative Image Studios for providing us with a playground for ten hours.

Thanks to Chelsea from Sundries and Plunder for creating a beautiful jackal mask for me.

Special thanks to Dr. Maya Angelou, Ivana Santilli, Daniela Saldias, Leonardo Mera, Warren Lordo, Hasan Ay, Juan Rios, Terry O'Neill, Michael Cordova, Nicholas Paige, Kevin Carvalho, James Gen Meers, LaToya Brathwaite, Scott Taylor, Angel Brazeau-Taylor, Tammy Dumont, Cindy and Bryan Pilon, Tami Sterling, Angela Reyes, Michael Olivo-Moore, Josh Davidson, Mari Sol Fernandez, Kezia Sinclair, Bruce and Julie Kurta, Darko Giacomini, Stella Emily Aird, Shoshana Klein, J.R. Dash, Jay Stewart, Paul Nicholas, Dawn Grace Laroza, Jesse Elliott, Quinn C Martin, Michael F. Paré, Thomas Gonder, Philip Cairns, Michael Erickson, Rogers TV, Mile High Underground.com, Buddies in Bad Times Theatre, Zelda's, Glad Day Bookshop, and The Press Club.

# Photographing Skeletons

*Tosin I. Arasi, president of TIA International Photography, specializes in capturing urban vistas and natural landscapes.*

Tosin I. Arasi, a Seattle-based photographer, has amassed a portfolio containing thousands of photos chronicling his visits to North American cities such as San Francisco, Los Angeles, Toronto, and Vancouver, as well as international cities such as Hong Kong, Macau, London, and Paris.

How does a photographer with a passion for capturing urban and natural wonders become the perfect choice to photograph a poet at his most vulnerable?

Kirk DeMatas explains, "I was already fairly familiar with Tosin's work as we have been close friends for years. When I was thinking about the artwork for my second book, I knew that I most certainly needed to work with a photographer who could get into my head, which also meant that I needed to work with someone I could trust. Tosin was the only logical choice. This project presented an opportunity for us to push ourselves artistically and personally, and I think we achieved what we set out to do."

Now, to delve further into the photography for *Conversations with Skeletons*, Tosin I. Arasi sits down with Kirk DeMatas to reflect over their first major collaboration.

**Kirk: Can you tell us what inspired you to transform your passion for photography into a business?**

**Tosin:** It took several years of convincing before I ventured into creating a small business for the photography. I have been taking photographs since I was a child, but it wasn't until my late twenties when I started to really take notice of the positive feedback and accolades from my family and friends for the images I had captured. They had seen something in my work that took me a while to personally appreciate. In March 2007, I was contacted by the City of Boston and informed that one of my photographs had been selected as a winner of their citywide photography competition. There were over four hundred entries, and only thirty-five pictures had been selected, one of which was my own. The significance behind this achievement was that I was the only non-resident of Boston to win. This was a fairly big occasion, as Mayor Thomas Menino himself was scheduled to present personal plaques to each of the photographers at an awards ceremony, which I was unable to attend due to my relocation from Washington, D.C., to Seattle. Regardless, that recognition was the trigger, the impetus. From that moment, I had become inspired to do more with my photography. I had a desire to travel more, visit more cities, capture these magnificent places on camera, and explore the world around me. By late 2009, I had finally developed the confidence to take the leap and the risk, to register my business with the City of Seattle as a sole proprietor, and TIA International Photography was born. Without the encouragement and support of my family and friends, including you, Kirk, TIA International would never have happened.

**Kirk: TIA International Photography is quickly building a global reputation for capturing breathtaking cityscapes, landscapes, and natural scenes. How challenging was it to photograph a living and breathing subject for the *Conversations with Skeletons* project?**

**Tosin:** That is an excellent question. When you initially approached me about the idea of doing the photography for *CWS (Conversations* *with Skeletons*), I was exhilarated and terrified at the same time. I was excited for the challenge and the scale of the project because it was completely foreign to my familiar comfort zone of capturing the personality of the different cities and urban landscapes, to which I was so well accustomed. However, there was a part of me that was frightened because I was engaging in such a personal and intimate project for one of my closest friends. The fear of failing to deliver excellent photography began to creep into my psyche, but I had to eliminate it over time simply for the reason that you had faith in me. Instinctively, you knew, well before I did, that I could handle the responsibility. You already knew that you wanted me, based in Seattle, to provide the photography when you could have gone with an unlimited number of photographers based locally in Toronto. Still, the challenge was always there for me. In my mind, failure was not an option because it meant a lot to me to be involved in *CWS*. I knew how much this book meant to you and how hard you had strived to create it. The advantage we had was our friendship. You and I are not strangers. We're more like brothers, and because of that relationship, I was more attuned to what you were trying to achieve when we started to discuss ideas several months in advance. That dynamic and synergy would not exist if we were not familiar with our respective personalities and the idiosyncrasies that come with them.

**Kirk: If you could choose one photo from *Conversations with Skeletons* that epitomizes the theme of this book, which photo would you choose and why?**

**Tosin:** I would have to say the shot of you crawling in the elevator. When we were shooting images in the old elevator lift at the studio, that was when I started to fully grasp the atmosphere, mood, vibe, and theme of *CWS*. You were playing a certain role, and I felt I was more than a photographer capturing the moment, which was significant. I was the observer, the reader, the viewer, and the pedestrian who crossed paths with your character. I began to ask myself while taking the photographs how I would feel if I were to suddenly encounter your character. I could fully perceive what it was you were communicating. Essentially, we were both in character, and I had a clear vision of what you wanted to convey to your audience. This particular image set the tone for me, which was towards the beginning of the photo shoot. I thought this was beneficial because I believe what you were trying to achieve had resonated with me, which led to a coherency I could maintain for all the other images. The synergy had always existed beforehand, during all our discussions and plans months in advance, but this image was my "I get it" moment. This image encapsulates and epitomizes *CWS* for me.

All photography for *Conversations with Skeletons* by Tosin I. Arasi/ TIA International Photography.
    To view more of Tosin's work please visit:
    www.tia-international-photography.com.

# Notes

The photograph on the book cover features the Sankofa symbol. The Sankofa, formulated by the Akan people of West Africa, teaches that we must travel back to the past and gather knowledge in order to create and claim an enriched future.

# About the Author

Kirk DeMatas is a poet and artist living in Toronto, and the author of the poetry collection *Wordspeak* (2008). As a committed advocate for the LGBT community, he interrupted the writing of his second book to pen the poem "NO H8" after becoming inspired by the American NO H8 Campaign. He quickly approached friend and artist/dancer/ producer Simone Maurice for assistance in bringing his poem to life. Maurice subsequently directed and produced five poetry shorts featuring DeMatas's recitation of the poem "NO H8," punctuated by the visual presence of Canadian artists, poets, and activists standing in unison against hatred.

In 2010, DeMatas made his first televised appearance on the Rogers Cable program "Toronto's Talent," reading poetry from his first book, *Wordspeak*. Since then, he has been featured at events such as Poetrix, an evening of poetry that was part of Toronto's 2012 PRIDE festival, and the 2nd Annual Hard & Able, an event organized by poet and performer Jay Stewart to celebrate those within the queer community living with disabilities. DeMatas has performed at world-famous venues such as Toronto's The Second City and Buddies in Bad Times Theatre. He continues to read his poetry at various events across the city of Toronto, as well as engage in collaborations with various artists on video poetry shorts, music, film and dance. He is currently working on his third poetry collection.

YouTube: @kirkspeak
Twitter: @kirkspeak